SLIP

SLIP

Amelia Loulli

CAPE POETRY

1 3 5 7 9 10 8 6 4 2

Jonathan Cape is part of the Penguin Random House group of companies
whose addresses can be found at global.penguinrandomhouse.com

Copyright © Amelia Loulli 2024

Amelia Loulli has asserted her right to be identified as the author of this
Work in accordance with the Copyright, Designs and Patents Act 1988

First published in the United Kingdom by Jonathan Cape in 2024

penguin.co.uk/vintage

A CIP catalogue record for this book is available from the British Library

ISBN 9781787334670

Typeset in 11/13pt Bembo Book MT Pro by Jouve (UK), Milton Keynes
Printed and bound in Great Britain by TJ Books Ltd, Padstow, Cornwall

The authorised representative in the EEA is Penguin Random House Ireland,
Morrison Chambers, 32 Nassau Street, Dublin D02 YH68

Penguin Random House is committed to a sustainable future
for our business, our readers and our planet. This book is made
from Forest Stewardship Council® certified paper.

love
is giving everything too easily
then staying to try and claw it back
Andrew McMillan

CONTENTS

III RAISING DAUGHTERS

EXPECT BLOOD

I'm going to tell you what happened
so you know
it was easy
so the memory becomes literal
like a leaf
I stayed awake
a tooth extraction
with less root
an injection
in the back of my hand
you'll have a bad head
like a good night
out the surgeon said
a small suction tube
removed
I slipped
out of myself
a short time sitting
on a blue leather chair
some biscuits
then home
except blood
there is no way around this
expect blood
liquid or solid
before it forms a skin
you will leave the clinic
singing
your arms will feel
like wings

I
GENESIS

The earliest written record of abortion is more than 4,000 years old.

*For me, words set down on paper to capture the thoughts and sensations
of a given moment are as irreversible as time — are time itself.*

Annie Ernaux

FOR MY CHILDREN

once   I caught a fish alive
six weeks   seven   eight nine ten

then   I let it go again
and you were with me   like water

when I fell into my own blood
covered the mirrors with handprints   red

one two buckle my shoe
you never forgot

the games we played
round and round the garden

your little fingers
showing me the church

and the steeple   *mummy*
look at all the people

how your singing hands
lifted me   *incy wincy spider*

carried this basket of apples
when *down came the rain and washed*

this body   my body
a church bell

crying   *me   me   me*
all the way

home again

COMING TO TERMS WITH OUR ABORTION
IN A TRACEY EMIN EXHIBITION

and I wore the clinic   like a cloak

wrapped myself in its dark   so my daughters kept asking
where I was   though I was always right there

like a grim black cat   and the clinic chair
became the only place I sat   and everywhere

was the waiting room   every bed
the theatre couch   and my hand was never free

of the tired nurse who held it   saying
that night she hoped to get home early   and my feet

were the glass screen   where they took my name
my head   was the scuffed corridor floor   black shoe stains

my arms were the walls   and all night I bled
the River Mersey   pissed water from the clinic taps

my hair became the ties   of the plastic waste bags   my eyes
the opaque containers   they put the babies in

THE UNPLANNED PREGNANCY HELPLINE

please hold   your call will be handled as soon as possible
we apologise for the delay   we are experiencing high call volumes at present

hello   you're speaking to operator twenty-five
the first human voice I've heard in days

there is so much I want to say
I know my call is important to you but do you know

some people believe in God's hands
there is no such thing as unplanned

no thank you   I would rather not
be contacted with details of fundraising events

I want to tell you all my children are at home
while I lay here in this rented room by the sea

talking to you   a black and white office calendar
draped over me   no   I can't do the 15th

I have to take my daughter to her piano exam
how many days will it take   to feel normal again

I can only eat tinned peaches and cheese
and I can tell you exactly how many songbirds

are papered onto these walls   yes I understand this call
is being recorded for training and quality purposes

I WILL WRITE THIS LIKE A BIRTH

because now you're listening
because now you're thinking about contractions

and the precision of a doctor who can slide their fingers
into a birth canal   and know   when a person will enter this world

about the opening of a pelvis   the sound of bones
something obvious about a rose   and yes

I was mostly naked   a wild thing   just how you imagine it
my hair wet with sweat   glittering   you know I howled

carnal animal   and you forgive me   of course
because this was natural   this bearing down   this purposeful

rhythmic breathing out   they held my hand
told me to squeeze   in my palms I felt a hundred heartbeats

the faces of nurses appearing above me   as though visions
and all the silence in the room   the swaying hush of hope

my body obeying this breach   and I so alive   I pushed
and here I am   still pushing

PORTRAIT WITHOUT A SONOGRAM

the woman   is indoors   on a lightless January day   she is on the
floor   in a cubicle   lights on   the woman is   in her kitchen
wearing   her dressing gown   wearing   a standard issue gown
tied at the back   the woman   has her back   to her washing machine
the woman is   the only person   in the room   she is   wearing a
pink gown   with insistent flowers   she is   sitting on the forest
floor   the woman   is laying on a bed   big enough   for only
her body   her hands in her lap   the woman is   in her kitchen
lights off   the woman   is in a room   made of blue   curtains
a glass of water   at her feet   the woman is   sleeping   under a
small   table on wheels   beside a tower   of three-a-day pill pots
the woman is   beside a broken   row of trees   the woman   has
red   cheeks   resting her head   on her washing machine   mid-
spin the woman is   far from the sea   wearing white socks   the
woman   is in her kitchen   wearing no rings   sleeping
under a whiteboard   her name   a date   the woman   has an
orange   skin marked   with the crescent indent   of her thumbnail
the woman   is waiting   for the painter   to finish she is sleeping
next to a chair   her bags and coat   the woman is   an animal who
didn't   run   she is   being   painted   with a blue cellular blanket
over her knees   the woman is   a target   resting   woundless
legs   the woman is lying   arms splayed open   dry lips   the
woman is   thinking   she will peel   the orange   the woman is
realising her insides   have all been removed   she can't eat   the
woman lies   her hands nowhere   near prayer   tongueless she
can't breathe   the woman is being   painted   palms up   hands
empty

GENESIS

What you decide on will be done, and light will shine on your ways.
Job 22:28

And the Bible doesn't mention us
not one of us women   not one mother
who   with germinating child   said no
we women who   with little flames
in our bellies   we women with candles
who drank turpentine   who threw
ourselves down forty stairs   leapt so high
we hit our heels on our own backsides
landed on bird spikes   pricked our inflated bellies
with pins   pulled out deflated skins on strings
we women who lay like fish   all night in the snow
baths full of ice cold   hung ourselves like fur coats
on wire hangers   we women who stepped over
vipers   swallowed gunpowder   not once did the Lord
God use his word   to praise us   to damn us   to name us

for whereof one cannot speak
thereof Lord   hear us

this is what we did

SONGS OF PRAISE I

if our mothers could see us now   corridor of girls lifting legs
like candles to the stirrups   eggshell gowns   blue ribbons

if they come
with their chants   if they come today   placards painted red

we could tell them
the surgeon is a priest   we could say Jesus
gave us the phone number for this place
he would pop round   wouldn't he

                                 he would

say a prayer   the sound of a Barbie doll
hitting the window   of a clinic

waiting room
                as holding cell

I'm saying the outside has horns
I'm talking mythical creature style horns
I'm saying the path out is dangerous with beasts
I'm talking bloodthirsty machines
I'm saying I feel like meat

LADY MARY OF THE ABORTION CLINIC

Our Lady of the immaculate conception
pray for us sinners   in the clinic
hidden beneath the basin   a statue
of Our Mother   our mothers
put her there   or their mothers
left her   on the tile floor
her head and her shoulders covered with dust
she stares at the wall   Mary
of the immaculate   red grouting
her bare feet wet   this is a perfect
cadence   the way each stone step has worn
into a downward slope at the edge
as though the place is tipping us out
us girls in single file fed through the place
like threads through cotton
she stands   in the dark bathroom
white gown pinched at the waist
hands always ready to reach for the light

MARY

I'm at this party being ignored   standing at the buffet while on the stage a man is cutting a pregnant woman's hair with an axe   I tell everyone motherhood is a country you can't leave   like this party but they are all spooning mayonnaise onto their plates   smiling   it's a Halloween party and I've come dressed as God   which offends some people who know him personally   faith is a mouth   I tell them as they eat sausage roll after sausage roll   I say last night I had a dream that Jesus was aborted   that Joseph promised Mary he would get her out of there   didn't matter how   that he would take her some place that they'd steal a car or a donkey if they had to   but he didn't show and Mary who was also my best friend came to me   appeared to me with her brown hair plaited in a halo   so I took her   I told her do not be afraid and the surgeon hovered at her feet   a messenger with a suction tube and the Jesus in her womb vanished without a trace   I'm telling this story but everyone is busy watching the pregnant woman kneeling on stage   hair draped over a wooden block   the axe feathering

THE LIVING

It was my son
capturing insects with tweezers
keeping them too long in jars
releasing their tough little bodies
like silver bullets   I told him no
I told him not us
we don't do things like this
he cried   I told him he's the kind
of boy who makes friends with all that is
living   I said this with one hand
over my own mouth   struggling to breathe
I said this   and I was bleeding

ARIA

I

this is how I fell for the clinic
its simple melody

the metronome   drip   drip   drip
of procaine

chanting childhood rhymes
Hey Diddle Diddle

I swallowed the fiddle
jumped all the way over the moon

with its arched back I was the cat
hissing a hollow tune

II

I'm a little vacuum tube
short and stout
misoprostol in
and pour me out

III

here are the lady's laminaria rods
here is the lady's table

here is the lady's speculum
and here is the tissue's cradle

SONGS OF PRAISE II

release as holding cell
coffee mornings with other mums from school

as holding cell

imagine a secret   *we all have secrets*   says Laraine who talks

openly about her divorce   body like an early text   discarded
Gina is a Christian who believes in love

but someone has to speak up for the babies   imagine the taste
 of twenty-five hand-iced fairy cakes   my vagina as fairy cake

Tinkerbell my mother called it   hundreds and thousands   what if
I said it
 there is an abortion counter online   tick tick tick   what if

I said I watch it   I'm not asking you to answer   Jesus
don't you know anything about the rhetorical   what if you   couldn't
what if you had to   what if you wanted to   think liberation
think feminism   I am bleeding into my office chair
soaking occurs post trauma

can you really say you're intimate with someone if you don't know
what they look like in the company of death   back to the fairy cakes
you wish this was sexier   if you want a ghost

to leave you alone   become as insignificant as a grey stone
jump   hit your heels against your tail bone a controlled fall into a
hot bath   the frog was covered with a white cheesecloth

then put inside my mouth   *hold it there   until it dies*   they said
        how will I know

you will feel its heart thumping between your lips   *when it stops*
you will know you have been cured

I left the clinic
a brick of padding between my legs

           I left my body
to the grey stone steps

      became a way in
and a way out

FAITH

I spent a year inside the word
GOD like a budget hotel room
I slept badly in its same four walls
my belongings thrown
over the brown furniture
listening to the creaks
and strange noises
watching the sunlight slip in
then drain back out again
there wasn't much to say
when a word limits itself
with such tight borders
a *G*   and a *D*   with the *O*
of the open mouth between
sometimes I forgot where I was
heard only part of the place   *GO*
GO   I wanted to   but my tongue
liked the earth of it   *God*
being somehow so close to *ground*   my tongue
the serpent   pulling itself around
the garden floor of it
I ate only variations
of things you can do with apples
and waited
when the bad things happened
I gasped   through god's open mouth
when I found the garden   empty as a throat
no plants no flowers no grass no seeds
no birds no butterflies no ants no bees
through god's empty throat I spoke
the new old words   their edges rough
to the touch   *trauma   grief   sin   a mother*
and her lost son   there is always a lost

son   god's empty mouth cannot contain us
the word was a room and the room was a kingdom
and the kingdom was lightless
an unlit body   needing water
needing air   what I mean is
I crawled out of god's open mouth

MOTHERING-ON

As another March
creeps into the barn
with its rain

the ewe is heavy
her udders engorged
she cannot eat dinner

so she takes herself away
to a corner where she delivers
two sweet lambs into this god-forsaken place

the blood-soaked hay sticks
to her legs   and she cries
for the third she can feel on the way

for this baby she cannot raise
there will be few options
the ewe may take it and dip it

in the juices of another mother's labour
try to fool her into thinking it's hers
or the farmer will take it

to a mother in grief
fix the coat of her dead
to its skin

HOLY WATER

So everything will live where the river goes.
Ezekiel 47:9

the river is on fire   somewhere near a moonless industrial unit
        in Merseyside   where they dispose of her remains
the river is pure paraffin   the river is a forest of flames
        a labyrinth of flammable swimming spots   the river
        will never be the same again   the river
has never known such heat   the river is more fluid now
        than it's ever been   the river is a rippling depth
of pyrotechnics   the river is blazing
        the river is incapable of putting itself out
an incendiary waterway   the river can set fire
        to this whole godforsaken place   the river is reflecting
its own brilliant orange blue   the river is a fire in a mirror
        a torch of veins   the river is a beautiful, monstrous truth
the river is a tinder box   dry with its own desperate retching
        don't you think it wants to bring even one tiny thing back?
don't you think God would be impressed by a whole body
        so sorry   so fierce it has learnt to become a fuel
to strike a match   to hold its own breath?

II
LITTLE RED

The wolf said, 'You know, my dear, it isn't safe for a little girl to walk through these woods alone.'

THE ABORTION

oh mother
what a big mouth
you have

all the better to swallow you with
my dear   slip of cells
for there is no science in the woods

only life provoking more life
the way love provokes more love
and what   did we expect

we slept with an axe
between us   while I grew
quickened with the truth

I was a wolf
and I lost Little Red
the way a mother loses a child

all of my wolf
blood draining
out of me

onto the floor
of a house
made of wood

PARTS OF A RIVER

dip your finger in a moving body
of water   watch
how the water struggles

to surround you and pass you   at the same time
watch   how if that finger   were a baby
it would always be   completely covered

and completely   left behind
Little Red was not given   or left   or loved
by water   yet   Little Red's mother

was a river   with a mouth   and a bed
Little Red hung   from her mother's mouth
like eel grass   *it was as though she gobbled me up*

it was as though   she swapped me with her tongue
so it was me   who hit the roof
of her mouth   every time she spoke

RED'S SONG

I'm on my way to Grandma's house
riding in my little red heart
bonnet full of sun
boot full of flowers
back seat jumping with jars of honey
this path of pins   busy with bees
my shiny black shoes on the gas
I'm not stopping for nobody
unless that nobody
knows all there is to know
about hearts

IN THE VOICE OF THE STORY I

Little Red's grandmother ate
microwavable macaroni cheese
called Little Red's mother *a waste of fucking space*

filled her cottage with balls and balls of black wool
rows of wool cabinets lined her walls
she had drawers full of knitting needles

on her arms she had the names of her children
and grandchildren and dead relatives tattooed
her arms read like a newspaper column

announcing births and deaths
she didn't know Little Red
belonged on her arm   twice

Little Red's mother used a knitting needle
to scratch her left elbow pit
the summer she was eight

when the plaster cast made her skin impossible
she dragged the cold metal stick
up and down her arm and felt

for the first time
something
like pleasure

IN THE VOICE OF LITTLE RED

Once upon a time
people believed my mother

was trying to kill me
she was feeding me strange leaves

with red veins and blue skin
but I was not afraid I asked

her who sent for me
three times she said

it *wasn't* me
it wasn't *me*

it wasn't me
spell broken

I kissed her
sank into

a body
of water

and even this
was not

the end

IN THE VOICE OF THE STORY II

let me tell you how it goes

once upon a time
her mother hadn't the heart

to scold her   hadn't the heart
to hold her   hadn't the heart

to lift her out of the car seat
alone   hadn't the heart

to say   at the lake a woman
sits folded at the waist

not knowing how to live in this world
with its girls jumping off roofs to save themselves

once a woman was killed by a circus clown
who picked her up by the ankles and swung her

round and round
she hadn't the heart to say

that everything male is made of glass
that the father is a windowpane

THE WOODCUTTER'S SONG

sing birch   sing pine
raise your voice like a roof

lay elm and oak for the wide axe stroke
sing a valley of unhewn blue

sweet maple and hazel and common beech
bring down the red bird cherry and weep

my willow   weep

FATHER?

In some versions
Little Red has a father
who wears lumberjack shirts
made of rough cotton
drives a heavy goods vehicle
has arms of thick timber
stands in the doorway of the cottage
so Little Red can't leave

in another version he flees
leaves the mother
alone in that bed
eating her own nails
picking at the skin on the insides
of her wrists   she makes lace
takes a drip stand with her
to clean her face

in another version he brings flowers
cut at a careful slant
he places their stems in cold water
leaves them by the bed
where he waits
for as long as it takes

IN THE VOICE OF THE WOLF

I was trying not to
I was taking pills
I'd forgotten the taste of blood
the feeling of arms and elbows
rippling my insides
revealing themselves like sticks
on the surface of a river
I was supposed to be safe
I'd stood amongst children
and not felt hungry
I'd been feeding myself
earthworms and birds
learned how to warm
my fur by the fire   to feel full
I'd held babies in my paws
and felt nothing
hadn't tasted flesh for years
yet there she was
easy as water she slipped
down the neck
soaked into everything

IN THE VOICE OF THE MOTHER:
AFTERWARDS

Funny
how a story
can get out of hand
become bigger than itself
become more pregnant than I ever was

I know stories of what people say
about women like me
I try not to tell them to myself
while I'm doing other things
like turning my mattress or tying my shoes

I try to see each day as its own
new story   I know who I was
I know you don't just shake off
being Little Red's mother

like an old skin
but I allow myself
to sit on the floor
of the woods sometimes

and notice
the columns of light
falling like trees
on countless beds of leaves

a robin   disturbing the ground
with its beak
how it seems to know exactly what it's doing
how it doesn't even notice me

WICKED

She will tell you about the time she caught a rabbit
held its trembling throat in one hand like a pint glass
peeled the skin and cut the flesh from its soft body
licked her fingers clean   everyone else at a christening
pouring holy water and wine   from bottles shaped
like newborn heads   she will tell you how Venus
is motherless   the butchered testicle of her father's body
how bones sound like seashells when they break
how little girls are disgusted by her smile   until one day
as grown women   they walk their own children in the woods
a rabbit! Mummy, look!   then starved and socket-eyed
they feel something vital   twitching

EL CAPPELIN ROSSO

two years later I lay in bed
a book in my lap –

Little Red Hat

an old Italian story I believe
has nothing to do with my own

I do all the voices

I am the grandmother   her intestines
strung up as a light pull

I am the mother who only wants
to walk a while in the woods with her child

I am the woodcutter
clutching the axe like a throat

I am the wolf   the better to end this
my dear   Little Red

are you listening?

the lights are out
and I cannot sleep

on my side of the bed
where I woke

all those red weeks with my
hands on my stomach

and the girl ate from her grandmother's flesh

and the girl drank from her mother's blood

and the girl climbed into bed with the wolf

I hadn't the heart
to hold you
so I took you

to where you could escape
the red tails
of your lovely coat
fleeing

III
RAISING DAUGHTERS

The woman who has felt 'unmothered' may seek mothers all her life.

Adrienne Rich

PIANO LESSONS

It took my mother four days
to chop the wood of the grand piano

small enough to burn   I was mid-Mozart
my fingers holding the next quaver run

like a breath   I might have forgotten how to play
if my teacher hadn't taught me   *anything can be*

a keyboard   a window ledge   a train table   your leg
where there is no music there is no joy   she said

while my mother sweated over steel strings
her axe striking the frame

in common time   I noticed
how even destruction has a song

I sat watching her   my fingers on my thighs
picking up her rhythm   playing along

MISS POLLY HAD A DOLLY

Yesterday I ate one of the dolls
she was rubbery and hard to chew

her small fists were bitter like cobnuts
and her eyelashes tickled my throat

I had to be brave when I swallowed her hair
it wasn't that there was nothing else to eat

it was that she wouldn't stop talking
about how long it's been since you last

sat here on my bed   she wouldn't stop
turning my hands over and over in hers

like playing cards palms up   palms down
face up face down she wouldn't stop

knowing what I know   I have your hands Mother
and I notice this most when I'm getting ready to eat

BOYS

first   she boarded an airplane
aged fifteen   left the country she grew up in
to go to school in the sticky heat of Georgia's south

watched the golden jocks in their cowboy hats
her mouth open   like an empty pantry
as she walked past their desks   in blue denim shorts

to sharpen her pencil   hoping to catch
their Davidoff Cool Water cologne on her tongue
but it was the minister's son

a boy of God   who touched her first
during Bible Study at his house   they snuck away
from the breakfast bread and scripture

to the couch in the basement   and so it came to pass
two angels on a white leather cloud   the new testament
echoing from the kitchen   that morning

when the holy spirit entered her
she did the only decent thing
she bowed her head   gave thanks

KISSING LESSONS

to touch or caress with the lips
as in the daughter kissed her mother on the cheek
but with complications as in did I kiss him
or did he kiss me   less than half of all cultures kiss
romantically   also a small cake biscuit or sweet
bring your own kisses   I burnt the kiss   he forgot
to put the sugar in   kiss of life   kiss of death   blow a kiss
through the air   if they don't respond they can kiss your dust
kiss goodbye   a slight touch of one against another
as in the bumper of your car kissed the boot of my car
we exchanged numbers for insurance purposes
seal it with a kiss   the true origin of kissing
remains a mystery   but the practice of rubbing noses
dates from 1500 BC   eventually someone slipped
discovered the lips   some say it began as most things do
with mothers feeding their young   she chewed the food
then pushed it into her child's mouth   swallowing
only the savour for herself

GIRLHOOD

I was a mother before I understood   anatomy
all those times I touched myself   clueless
said my stomach hurts while pointing at my   uterus

swear on the uniform handbook   girls are forbidden
from wearing trousers   a ruler will be used
to measure the journey from knee to hem   four of his fingers

and afterwards   I shook   went alone
to the fairground   ate bread crusts dipped in sugar
the walls were mirrors   and the red leather booth
    stuck to my legs

TWO CENTIMETRES DILATED

I watch
a man
jump
a hundred and twenty
thousand feet
in freefall
from space
just trying
to get close
to understanding
how this feels
the stupid size
of this
hurtling
towards earth
at speeds
untested
to carry
something
soft as an oyster
unknown
as a star
inside
to be
the protector
of all that
life
that slightness
of flesh
to depend
only
upon a cord
oh Lord

and the whole world
waits
for the man
to land
and all the while
unwatched
I open

BROKEN WATERS

Most people drown
   without making
a noise or splashing. See me

here Baby, watch
    me lying
like a plank, below the surface,

all that stillness, all that
      peace, see
how long I can breathe

down here alone. You must
     trust me,
I am your mother after all,

don't think about the firefighter
     who lies
to the woman on the phone inside

the burning building, says he's on his
     way up
to save her, then hands her brother

back the phone, *tell her you*
    love her,
knowing all his tears

won't be enough to quiet the
    flames, I am
your mother after all, I am made

to do this. When the mother harp seal

leaves its cub,
nobody calls it a mistake,

I have been at this much longer than
            twelve days,
just let me float here a while, Baby

you will still remember my face,
            it will be
the same one you wear every time

life cuts in such a way, the undertow
            drags the exact
formation of ripples across its shape.

YOUR FIRST YEAR   MISREMEMBERED

we woke each other   slowly
every morning like blossom

opening ourselves to the waiting sun
I fed you easily   while the rain was missing

from that scorched summer   my friends couldn't believe
how free I seemed   you were as glue to a marriage

your daddy and me   we ate happily
three-hundred-and-sixty-five candle-lit dinners

while you slept in a basket   like a bright yield
of fresh fruit at our feet   always sweet

your first word was a song
you held me with your tiny hands

wrapped round my fingers like gold rings
you were content to lay back counting sheep

and when I went to the doctor
he held you   as we sang for him

our aria of pure delight
at having born each other

after listening   carefully
he told us to stay   for as long as we liked

brought in a tray of finger sandwiches
and fairy cakes   *this is a party*

he said   *and you are my honoured guests*
so we did not go home   and weep and weep

ELEGY FOR A YEAR

I was twenty-three
there was more snow that year

than any other year
I had three small children

and no car
I wore two coats

in the house   kept myself
always moving

from the log pile to the stove
it was the year I learned to loathe

the pigeons and their doleful
death-filled moans

I axed the wood
and shuffled the baskets

and closed the doors
loudly   to drown out

those hateful birds
I lit candles and told stories

about snowflakes and icicles
and bonfires and apples

while the long winter stretched
its never-ending spine

across the village
that year we lived

a snow globe
all those slow young days

wide eyes   big open mouths
multiple snowflakes

brisk as the endless bright ice
my body longed for escape

I was twenty-three
and the year shook me

BED FOURTEEN

the appendix belongs in the abdomen
until it bursts

and the daughter's body belongs
on the surgeon's table

plastic tube inside her open mouth
knife in his hand

camera threaded through bellybutton
made when they cut the cord

I have belonged for a week
to bed fourteen of the rainbow ward

drawing a room of our own
with my body and a bright blue curtain

pouring water from a plastic jug
into disposable paper cups

watching her swelling stomach
and a contracting moon

belonging in the frame
of the unwashed hospital window

tending cries in the night like the newborn
pain   that slippery   howling

until they catch it   take bed fourteen
to theatre   all the world her stage   and I

belonging   in the blue plastic chair
beneath the absent   clock moon

realise   her face tells lies
making us believe we all have time

that what we love will always
return

SLIP

where have you gone   little slip
of cells   what are you now   a flower   next spring?

before and after you   I keep a list of all I'm thankful for
cardigans   music   truth   the boy who would have been

your brother gets his hair cut   tells the barber he wants less
than more   his hair on the floor   *soap*

apples   I can't shower   the smell
of the clinic   the sight of my skin   but there is

cherry jam   clean washing   from inside me
a collection tube   into an opaque container labelled   with my name

pregnancy remains are regarded   as the tissue of the woman

my arms   a safe place to sleep   blood still giving way
I lean myself against my bedroom wall listen to the storm
rain soaking   the brick   staining red

my hands on the inside   almost touching   almost owning
the water as it falls

COLLEGE BUS STOP

I slipped into the wet darkness to get you
daughter   that winter evening   the nesting
birds   the stars   the moon   no comfort
only the struggling light of day   too far

too waning   I walked unsteady on the ice
the long straight lane ahead of me   the unseeable
end being you   I knew   which is why I kept pushing
forward   past the still body waiting in its own silhouette

on the corner   past the houses locked with night
I wanted to get there before you did
to be a Good Mother   to be there and ready
to receive you   but I moved too slowly

lost my step   while at the bottom of the soaked road
you arrived   unconcerned   taking out the torch
you keep in your bag   you began
walking   waving your illuminated hand at me

stopped in the dark   fixed on your light
I watched you come quickly to meet me
and wondered at how hard it was
to let that be

CAN YOU DESCRIBE THE PAIN?

carrying a pocket of infection in my left cheek
my face swells   to match my mother's
swollen face   all those times I came home from school
to find her bruised   and the furniture all moved
to the middle of the living room   I never looked
in the mirror and saw her   until now
rounded creature-like cheeks   I always wondered why
she moved the furniture so silently   the dentist tells me
to raise my right hand if the rod he is inserting into my tooth
hurts   I lift my hand   he takes the rod out of my mouth
and asks me to describe the pain   I see my mother
dragging the dresser and the sofa across the carpet and realise
how much language fails to describe the way we hurt
even now   what can I say   my mouth is sore/sharp/stabbing
my mouth is tender/suffering   my mouth is throbbing/aching/pulsing
but these words are always the same   I try again   my mouth
is pressure   head in a vice   hot   banging   a needle   a rock
shattered glass   a cake made of sand   hit by a bus
my mouth is a bowl of bees   a cup of fire ants   the foundation
of a building being hit with brick after brick   my mouth is full
of canals   my mouth is a bookshelf being kicked
by my mother's feet   my mouth is a piano being dragged
by its keys   afterwards my mother always sat on an armchair
in the centre of the room   surrounded by the chaos she had created
she would close her eyes   then begin   to put it all back again

MRS THOROGOOD

my heart   is the textbook my piano teacher wrote
by hand and gave to me   *in case you ever need it*

in case I ever needed a hand-written book explaining
the technicalities of common and cut common time

in case I woke up one day   and realised I needed her
handwriting to tell me   the structure of the diminished

seventh   fell ill and needed her notation to illustrate
the moment   a harmony note becomes dissonant

with a new chord   becoming a suspension
and she was right

twenty years later   when all the music I had learned from her
grew bleak   when my heart had become a car park

at the back of an old hotel   I needed her
words   written always in thin silver pencil   her heart

the purple felt tip pen   underlining
every   most   important   thing

AFTER A VIOLATION

winter   and my daughter
is sitting on our garden bench
with a telescope   asking me how
to focus the moon   she doesn't know
why I've been inside   for so long
how bodies can need   hiding
so she begged me out here   and I am cold
watching her   head bowed
to the scope   studying the dials and levers
we don't understand   and I'm about to go in
tell her there is nothing   worth waiting for
in this darkness   when she tells me
she's got it *look*   and she holds my face
to a half-wedge   of milk moon
the image is hazy   like an ultrasound
a small piece of body   we can celebrate
saying *I see you*   loving this world enough
to look

WHILE I WAS FEEDING YOU

the sexless years were all   breasts
they were all

flopping cracked nipples   in front of parting
lips   all oral   all reflex

they were all   between-meal jumpers
bundled half-mast   flashes   of skin

top-section-only   desperate
meetings of impropriety   eyes

for no other   all hunger and thirst
they were spent

the way I was   drop   by   drop
into another's mouth   mostly

horizontal   always
in love

NOTES FROM MY CHILDHOOD

The doll
was buried
with a note
folded up
inside her
dress   it was
from my mother
the note
it said
I didn't
realise
it would be
so difficult
to live
after
your brother
they cut it
out of me
all that
weaponry

AVE MARIA CONCERTO

I walked six miles to the church

her voice filled the roof
as she sang me back through the clinic

outside Rome roared
but my body was still in Liverpool

not knowing when to make the sign of the cross
I had the sky's blue all over my hands

like ink from the consent forms   afterwards I told her
I learned Ave Maria on the piano when I was a child

and my mother actually liked it
she hugged me   as though I were still bleeding

she cried too   when I told her it was all so beautiful
she spoke like a kind doctor in soft Italian

I was wearing a bracelet
covered with pictures of the Virgin Mary

which I bought for one euro
from a souvenir shop

IN ROME, I MISS MY MOTHER MORE THAN EVER

in every column every frame every canvas every saint
here   there is a mother

in the piazzas holding their bowls of open space
from the long narrow roads of the city

and the fountains choked with strangers
dipping their fingers in the green waters   mothers

in every sculpture every garden every rafter
sitting on the steps of another needle   there is her softness

in the stone   the domestic routine of the parrots
screaming their way to nest at dusk   the alarm

raised by the birds shapeshifting over the river
black glitter   I am always at my mother's funeral

since the winter she stopped looking at me for good
even the traffic is processional   like the loveless

scoops of ice cream I buy myself day after day
knowing there is sweetness only in the mother of every church

standing perfectly still in their perfect skirts   in every doorway
Santamaria   Our Lady   Madonna   for every shop front

a blessing for getting all you want   there is a mother
in the thin white sheets layered on the beds at night

in the medicine I cannot find   there is a mother
in every crucifix   every organ   every crypt

in every window seared   with a hot blue sky
there is a mother   but never mine

EPILOGUE FOR MY DAUGHTERS

Should you ever find yourself
in the early hours of an unwanted morning
dawn pressing its advent into your sky
sunrise crowing its first light   it is always yours
to know what you will   and what you will not
and should you not want to   then love of course

you do not have to carry anything for this world
you are not space   you are not waves   you are no
vessel   no receptacle   no basin   no jug   no barrel
no casket   no urn   no drum   you are solid
rooted flesh   circuited blood
belonging here   on this hallowed ground

and should you ever hear yourself pray
to a God you don't believe exists   who chooses
not to answer   then my love   hear this

yes

to every sacred thing you wish

ACKNOWLEDGEMENTS

Thanks to the editors of the following publications, where some of these poems have appeared: *After Sex*, *The Forward Book of Poetry 2023*, *London Review of Books*, *Poetry Review*, *Primers Volume IV*, *The Rialto*, *Under the Radar Magazine*, and to New Writing North for the Northern Writers' Award which afforded me the time to finish this manuscript as well as the chance to work with my poetry hero, Fiona Benson.

This book is dedicated to my children, who have shown me what it is to be a part of a family built on love, trust, good humour and the never-ending book of 'things we're grateful for', which we keep on the kitchen table and add to, even in the toughest times. Sophia, Nico and Elena – the book we're writing together, listing our gifts, is the best book I'll ever have. Thank you for loving me.

To all the writers who have shown me what poetry can do: every one of you appears in my list of gifts more than once: Tara Bergin, Jacob Polley, Sinéad Morrissey, Victoria Richards, Kate Walford, Kim Moore, Jenny Valentine, Jane Commane, Kim Addonizio, Linda France, Daljit Nagra, Clare Pollard, Ella Frears, Alice Oswald; and to my agent, Becky Thomas, for being excited enough about my work to sign me. Thanks especially to the inimitable Caroline Bird for reading an early draft of the manuscript and making it better; and to Andrew McMillan, whose work sent me with full force into becoming a poet. One day I might even become one. Thank you to Robin Robertson for calling me up one December evening and changing my life. Your vast wisdom and attention to my work has been a wonder. I will always be grateful. Finally – dear Fiona, you are in every page of this book. The year I spent working with you can only have been the best dream. Your beautiful generosity, tender insight, and your own phenomenal work have made this book, and so much more, possible for me. Thank you.